# KNOW ABOUT
# ALBERT EINSTEIN

MAPLE KIDS

KNOW ABOUT ALBERT EINSTEIN

Published by

MAPLE PRESS PRIVATE LIMITED
office: A-63, Sector 58, Noida 201301, U.P., India
phone: +91 120 455 3581, 455 3583
email: info@maplepress.co.in
website: www.maplepress.co.in

Reprinted in 2019

ISBN:978-93-50334-19-5

# Contents

# Preface

Albert Einstein is undoubtedly one of the most fascinating and influential figures of the modern era. As a pre-eminent physicist, he thoroughly transformed people's understanding of the universe. As an ardent humanist, he took an active and outspoken stance on the significant political and social issues of his time. As a committed Jew, he advocated a distinctive moral role for the Jewish people.

Albert Einstein's contribution to modern Physics is simply unique. His scientific career was a constant quest for the universal and immutable laws, which govern the physical world. His theories spanned the fundamental questions of nature, from the very large to the very small, from the cosmos to sub-atomic particles. He overturned the established concepts of time and space, energy and matter. Einstein played a crucial role in establishing the two pillars of 20th century Physics. He was the father of the theory of relativity and a major contributor to quantum theory.

# CHAPTER 1
# Early Years

Science was Albert Einstein's first love, yet he always found time to devote tireless efforts to political causes close to his heart. His ardent humanism led him to strive for peace, freedom and social justice. The young Einstein found the authoritarianism and militarism of the German educational system profoundly disturbing. The virulent nationalism and brutality of the First World War served to confirm Einstein's pacifist and internationalist convictions. Einstein was not a purely abstract thinker. He grasped the world in concrete images and strove to translate them into words and equations that could be understood by others.

Albert Einstein was born on March 14, 1879, in Germany. In 1880, the year after Einstein's birth, his family moved from Ulm to Munich, where Hermann Einstein, his father and Jakob Einstein, his uncle, setup a small electrical plant and engineering works. In Munich, Einstein attended rigidly disciplined schools. Under the harsh and pedantic regimentation of 19th century German education, which he found intimidating and boring, he showed little scholastic ability.

At the behest of his mother, Einstein also studied music.

Though throughout life he played exclusively for relaxation, he became an accomplished violinist. It was during this period that Uncle Jakob stimulated in Einstein a fascination for mathematics and Uncle Casar Koch stimulated a consuming curiosity about Science.

Albert's inquisitive nature was revealed from an early age. As a small boy, he was self-sufficient and thoughtful. When he was four or five years old, his father gave him a magnetic compass. He was impressed by the needle's invariable northward swing, which he thought was guided by an invisible force. After analysing the compass for a while, he came to the conclusion that there had to be 'something behind things, something deeply hidden'.

During his formative years, Einstein was a slow talker. He would often pause to consider what he intended to say. His uncle, an engineer and a medical student, who once ate at his place, stimulated his thoughts that directed the course of his life, thereafter.

In his own words, "At the age of 12, I experienced a wonder in a booklet dealing with Euclidean plane geometry, which came into my hands at the beginning of a school year. Here were assertions, as for example, the intersection of the three altitudes of a triangle at one point, which though by no means evident - could nevertheless be proved with such certainty that any doubt appeared to be out of the question. This lucidity and certainty made an indescribable impression on me."

# CHAPTER 2
# Graduation

At school, Albert seldom got good grades. However, he acquired outstanding grades in mathematics. He hated the academic high school and was sent to Munich. Success at this school depended on memorisation and obedience to arbitrary authority. It was his home, where he studied Mathematics, Physics and Philosophy extensively. On account of his bad grades, one of his teachers suggested him to leave the school. According to him, Einstein's presence destroyed the other students' respect for the teacher.

Consequently, at the age of fifteen, he quit the school in mid-term. Thereafter, he joined his parents, who had moved to Italy.

In 1895, Einstein took the entrance examination for the Swiss Federal Institute of Technology. He failed in the exam and was advised to study at a Swiss school in Aarau. At the new school, his teachers were humane and his ideas were set free.

His thoughts turned to the theory of electromagnetism formulated by James Clerk Maxwell.

At the age of 16, Einstein wrote an essay in French, in which he explained his fondness for studying theoretical Mathematics or Physics.

*Einstein's essay for the Aarau school, written in French.*

"A happy man is too content with the present to think much about the future. On the other hand it is young people, above all, who like to occupy themselves with bold plans.... If I should have the good fortune to pass my examinations, I would go to the Zurich polytechnical school. I would stay there for four years in order to study Mathematics and Physics. I see myself becoming a teacher in these branches of the natural sciences, choosing the theoretical part of these sciences.

Here are the reasons that led me to this plan. Above all it is my individual disposition for abstract and Mathematical thought... And then there is a certain independence in the scientific profession which greatly pleases me."

Einstein graduated from the Aarau School and entered the Institute of Technology in Zurich. Around this time, he recognised that physics was his true subject. Only there could he seek out the paths that led to the depths. He also realised that he could never be an outstanding student. Einstein met Marcel Grossmann, Gustav Geissler and Eugen Grossmann in Zurich.

Marcel Grossmann quickly recognised his friend's genius. He did all he could to promote Einstein's career. Fortunately, Marcel Grossmann had the conventional traits that Einstein lacked. While Einstein worked in the library or the laboratory, Grossmann took excellent notes at the mathematics lectures and gladly shared them with his friend before examinations. Einstein later wrote, "I would rather not speculate on what would have become of me without these notes."

# CHAPTER 3
# Getting a Job

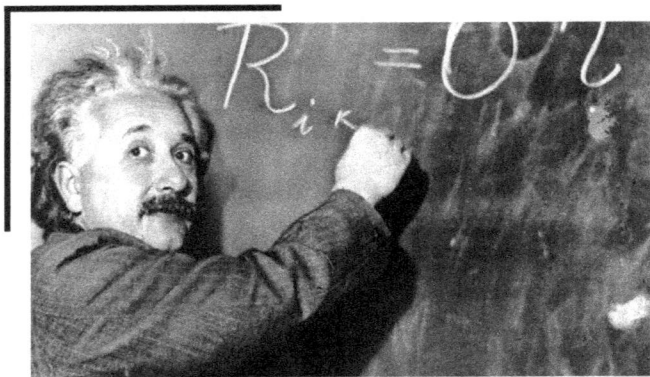

Einstein grew familiar with the successes of past scientists who had tried to explain the world entirely through atoms or fluids, interacting like parts of a machine. But he learned that Maxwell's theory of electricity and magnetism was defying efforts to reduce it to mechanical processes. Through a new friend, the engineer Michele Besso, Einstein came to the writings of Ernst Mach. He was a skeptical critic of accepted ideas in Physics.

After Einstein graduated with an undistinguished record, he made a number of efforts to get a university job. However, he failed in his efforts. He found only occasional jobs on the periphery of the academic world. He felt he was a burden on his none too prosperous family and wondered if he had been mistaken in trying to become a physicist.

Finally, Einstein got a position at the Swiss Patent Office in Bern. It was 'a kind of salvation,' he said. The regular salary and the stimulating work evaluating patent claims freed Einstein. He now had time to devote his thought to the most basic problems of Physics of his time. In addition, he began to publish scientific papers.

Einstein's closest friend was Michele Besso, with whom he would walk back home from the Patent Office, discussing his scientific thoughts and ideas. Einstein thought of him as 'the best sounding board in Europe for his scientific ideas'. With other friends in Bern, all unknown to the academic world, Einstein met regularly to read and discuss books on Science and Philosophy. They called themselves the Olympia Academy, mocking the official bodies that dominated science.

Einstein began to attract respect with his published papers. In 1909, he was appointed as an associate professor at the University of Zurich.

He was also invited to present his theories before the annual convention of German scientists. He met many people he had known only through their writings, such as the physicist Max Planck of Berlin. Soon Einstein was invited to the German University in Parague as full professor. Here he met a visiting Austrian physicist, Paul Ehrenfest. "Within a few hours we were true friends," Einstein recalled, "as though our dreams and aspirations were made for each other."

# CHAPTER 4
## Mileva Maric

At the Zurich Polytechnic, a romance arose between the handsome and witty would be Science teacher and a young Serbian woman, Mileva Maric, the only woman in Albert's Physics class. Mileva Maric's life was a jigsaw puzzle. On the one side, Einstein was a scientific saint and accepting Mileva as his equal would be blasphemous. On the other side, there is solid proof that Albert treated his wife disgracefully, raising the suspicion that he viewed Mileva's career with equal disregard.

Mileva Maric was born just before Christmas. At the time of birth, she suffered from a displaced hip. As a youngster, she showed a gift for Math and Languages, painting and music. Mileva's family was fairly wealthy and she received superior schooling.

When Mileva turned 15, her father got special permission for her to take classes at an all-male prep school. At school, she earned the highest grades in both Math and Physics. To continue her education, Mileva went to Zurich, one of the few European cities with a university that accepted women.

In 1896, she began studying medicine. By October, she was switched to the university's Technical Institute (ETH). She was nearly 21 and only the fifth woman to be accepted by the ETH. One of her classmates was Albert Einstein. He was 17, a boy barely worth noticing.

Mileva's first year was an academic success. But she started her second year with a semester in Heidelberg. Mileva and Albert exchanged letters while she was away. She described, in great detail, the satisfactions of her studies. In return, Albert called her a 'little runaway', telling her to 'come back soon'.

She returned and by 1899, all formalities were gone. Albert called her Dollie. She dubbed him Johnny. They embarked on a 'modern' love affair. Her parents were tolerant, knowing that Mileva's marital prospects were few, due to her intelligence and disability. Albert's parents opposed the relationship at every level. She was too old, too bookish, lame, a Slovene, not Jewish.

The greater the opposition, the more Mileva protected Einstein, eventually placing his interests before her own. He demanded all her time. She sacrificed her studies as well as her friends. In 1900, they both failed their final exams. Albert somehow got a diploma, but was one of the few graduates without a job. While he looked for work, she supported him emotionally and financially.

Nearly a year later, Albert went to his family in Italy. Maric stayed in Zurich, working as a lab assistant and preparing to retake her exams. In May, the couple rendezvoused at Lake Como for 3 or 4 days. Several weeks later, Mileva discovered that she was pregnant. In late January 1902, Mileva gave birth to Lieserl, at home in Novi Sad. Albert never went to see the child.

# CHAPTER 5
# Marriage

As 1902 came to a close, Mileva turned 27. By that time, she had become a family disgrace, an academic failure and mother of an illegitimate child. Albert was 23 and an employee of the Swiss Patent Office in Bern.

Finally, Albert and Mileva got married at Bern City Hall on January 6,1903. The marriage began with Einstein working 6 days a week at the Patent Office and spending his free time on

Physics. Mileva tried to cope with the loss of her career and her daughter, which she gave up for adoption. Just before their second anniversary, the Nobel Prize in Physics was awarded to Marie and Pierre Curie, a stinging reminder that Mileva once hoped for a career.

However, the next year went well. Albert got a raise. Mileva gave birth to a baby, Hans Albert. Mileva told a Serbian friend, "we finished some important work that will make my husband world famous." It was Einstein's *annas mirabilis*, the miracle year. Four papers were published and the science was astounding.

Through letters, visits and Science meetings, Einstein came to be known as one of the major physicists of Europe, which were not many in those days. As early as 1907, while Einstein and other scientists were exploring the implications of his special theory of relativity, he was already thinking about a more general theory. The special theory had shown how to relate the measurements made in one laboratory to the measurements made in another laboratory moving in a uniform way with respect to the first laboratory. He saw a possible link between such accelerated motion and the familiar force of gravity. He was impressed by a fact known to Galileo and Newton, but not fully appreciated before Einstein puzzled over it. All bodies, however different, if released from the same height will fall with exactly the same constant acceleration (in the absence of air resistance). Like the invariant velocity of light on which Einstein had founded his special 'Theory of Relativity', here was an invariance that could be the starting point for a theory.

In 1912, Einstein was invited back to the Swiss Federal Institute of Technology as a professor. Here, he rejoined his old friend Marcel Grossmann, who had become professor of Mathematics. With Grossmann's aid, Einstein studied the Mathematical theories and techniques, which he found necessary for his work towards a new theory of Gravitation. Meanwhile, Einstein was being introduced to a different sort of world by another friend,

Friedrich Adler. This time, Einstein's attention was directed towards the world of the Second International and its attempt to halt the growth of international rivalries in Europe.

In 1914, the German government gave Einstein a senior research appointment in Berlin, along with a membership in the prestigious Prussian Academy of Sciences. When Einstein had left his native land as a youth, he had renounced German citizenship and the entire militarist German society. But Berlin, with no teaching duties and a galaxy of top scientists for colleagues, could not be resisted. It was the highest level a scientific career could ordinarily reach.

"With such fame, not much time remains for his wife," Mileva complained. "I am very starved for love." Einstein felt suffocated in the increasingly strained and gloomy relationship. He found solace in a love affair with his cousin, Elsa Lowenthal.

# CHAPTER 6
# Papers published
# by Einstein During 1905

*March 1905*

Early in 1905, Einstein published in the prestigious German Physics monthly *Annalen der Physik*, a thesis, "A New Determination of Molecular Dimensions," that won him a Ph.D. from the University of Zurich. Four more important papers appeared in Annalen that year and forever changed man's view of the universe.

In the paper, Einstein proposed the idea that light could act as though it consists of discrete, independent particles of energy, in some ways like the particles of a gas. Max Planck suggested a similar idea a few years earlier . He was the first to suggest discreteness in energy. However, Einstein carried the idea much beyond this. He made a revolutionary proposal that contradicted the universally accepted theory that light consists of smoothly oscillating electromagnetic waves. Einstein showed that the particles of energy could help to explain the phenomena being studied by experimental physicists. In his paper, he clearly explained how light can eject electrons from metals. Einstein discovered light quanta by pondering experiments on particles discovered only a few years earlier.

*May 1905*

The *Annalen der Physik* received another paper from Einstein. The well-known kinetic energy theory explained heat as an effect of the ceaseless agitated motion of atoms. Einstein proposed a way to put the theory to a new and crucial experimental test. If tiny but visible particles were suspended in a liquid, he said, the irregular bombardment by the liquid's invisible atoms should cause the suspended particles to carry out a random jittering dances. Biologists had long since observed just such a random dance of microscopic particles. Einstein explained the motion in detail.

## *June 1905*

Einstein sent the *Annalen der Physik* a paper on electromagnetism and motion. Since the time of Galileo and Newton, physicists had known that laboratory measurements of mechanical processes could never show any difference between an apparatus at rest and an apparatus moving at constant speed in a straight line. Objects behave the same way on a uniformly moving ship as on a ship at the dock. This is called the Principle of Relativity.

Einstein had long been convinced that the Principle of Relativity must apply to all phenomena, mechanical or not. Now he found a way to show that this principle was compatible with electromagnetic theory after all. As Einstein later remarked, reconciling these seemingly incompatible ideas required 'only' a new and more careful consideration of the concept of time. His new theory, later called the special theory of relativity, was based on a novel analysis of space and time. The analysis is so clear and revealing that it can be understood by the beginning science students.

*September 1905*

Einstein reported a remarkable consequence of his special 'Theory of Relativity'. If a body emits a certain amount of energy, then the mass of that body must decrease by a proportionate amount. The paper was mathematical footnote to the special 'Theory of Relativity' and it established the equivalence of mass and energy, according to which the energy E of a quantity of matter, with mass m, is equal to the product of the mass and the square of the velocity of light, c. The relationship is expressed in an equation:

$$E = mc^2$$

# CHAPTER 7
# Second Marriage

Mileva and Albert separated in 1914 after bitter arguments and divorced in 1919.That same year, he married Elsa and settled in with her and her two daughters by a previous marriage. "The Lord has put into him so much that's beautiful and I find him wonderful," Elsa later wrote, "even though life at his side is enervating and difficult." Einstein enjoyed flirting with female admirers. A couple of times, he had passionate affairs. Elsa, despite bouts of jealousy and loneliness, guided him through his daily routines like a mother caring for a thoughtless child. After Elsa's death in 1936, her daughter, Margot, joined Einstein's secretary in the task of protecting Einstein from intrusions and helping him cope with everyday life.

As he often did in his work, Einstein used a 'thought experiment'. Suppose that a scientist is enclosed in a large box somewhere and that he releases a stone. The scientist sees the stone fall to the floor of the box with a constant acceleration. He might conclude that his box is in a place where there is a force of gravity pulling downward. But this might not be true. The entire box could be free from gravity, but accelerating upward in empty space on a rocket; the stone could be stationary and the floor rising to meet it. The physicist in the box cannot, Einstein noted, tell the difference between the two cases. He concluded that there must be some profound connection between accelerated motion and the force of gravity. It remained to work out this connection.

Einstein began to search for particular equations. The search was arduous, with entire years spent in blind alleys. Einstein had to master more elaborate Mathematical techniques than he had ever expected to need and to work at a higher level of abstraction than ever before.

Einstein's friend Michele Besso gave crucial help here. Meanwhile, The First World War broke out and he began to participate in politics.

Success in Einstein's theoretical work was sealed in 1915. The new equations of gravitation had an essential logical simplicity, despite their unfamiliar mathematical form. To describe the action of gravity, the equations showed how the presence of matter warped the very framework of space and time. This warping would determine how an object moved. Einstein tested his theory by correctly calculating a small discrepancy in the motion of the planet Mercury, a discrepancy that astronomers had long been at a loss to explain.

# CHAPTER 8
# International Acclaim

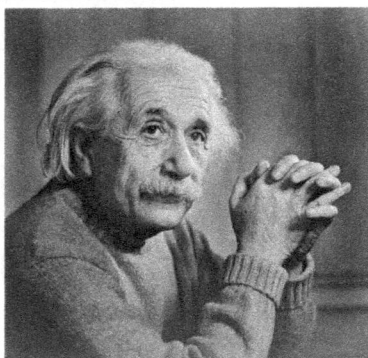

Einstein's new general Theory of Relativity predicted a remarkable effect. As per the theory, a ray of light bends as it passes near a massive body. Einstein clarified the theory with the example of starlight passing near the sun. He said that the starlight should be slightly deflected by gravity as it reaches near the sun. This deflection could be measured when the light rays from the sun were blocked during an eclipse.

Einstein predicted a specific amount of deflection and the prediction spurred British astronomers to try to observe a total eclipse. As a result, international fame came to Einstein in November 1919, when the Royal Society of London announced that its Scientific Expedition to the Island of Príncipe, in the Gulf of Guinea, had photographed the solar eclipse on May 29 of that year and completed calculations that verified the predictions made in Einstein's general theory of relativity.

In a letter to an astronomer in 1913, Einstein predicted how gravity should deflect rays of light that passed near the sun, making stars appear to shift their positions. In photographs taken by expeditions to an eclipse of the sun, the apparent positions of stars near the sun deviated from the positions of stars photographed when the sun was elsewhere in the sky. A ripple in a pane of glass can be detected when objects seen through the glass appear distorted. So scientists detected a warping of space itself.

Announcement of the eclipse results caused a sensation world over. It brought home to the public a transformation of physics, by Einstein and others that was overturning established views of time, space, matter and energy. Einstein became the world's symbol of the new physics. Some journalists took a perverse delight in exaggerating the incomprehensibility of his theory, claiming that only a genius could understand it. More serious thinkers like philosophers, artists, ordinary educated and curious people, took the trouble to study the new concepts. These people too, chose Einstein as a symbol for thought at its highest. In his words, "I have become rather like King Midas, except that everything turns not into gold but into a circus." Only a few could understand relativity, but the basic postulates were so revolutionary and the scientific community was so obviously bedazzled that the physicist was acclaimed the greatest genius on Earth. Einstein himself was amazed at the reaction and apparently displeased, for he resented the consequent interruptions of his work. On one occasion, he said, "Since that deluge of newspaper articles, I have been so flooded with questions, invitations, suggestions, that I keep dreaming I am roasting in Hell and the mailman is the devil eternally yelling at me, showering me with more bundles of letters at my head because I have not answered the old ones."

# CHAPTER 9
# The Pacifist Sympathies

With the start of the First World War, the political situation in Germany deteriorated. Einstein began attacking nationalism and promoted pacifist ideals. With the rising tide of anti-Semitism in Berlin, Einstein was castigated for his 'Bolshevism in physics' and the fury against him in right-wing circles grew, when he began to publicly support the Zionist movement. Judaism had played little part in his life, but he insisted that, as a snail can shed his shell and still be a snail, so a Jew can shed his faith and still be a Jew.

Ninety-three leading German intellectuals, including physicists such as Planck, signed a manifesto defending Germany's war conduct. Einstein and three others signed an antiwar counter-manifesto. He helped to form a non-partisan coalition that fought for a just peace and for a supranational organisation to prevent future wars. As a Swiss citizen, Einstein could feel free to spend his time on theoretical physics, but he kept looking for ways to reconcile the opposing sides. "My pacifism is an instinctive feeling," he said, "a feeling that possesses me because the murder of men is disgusting. My attitude is not derived from any intellectual theory but is based on my deepest antipathy to every kind of cruelty and hatred."

Along with Germany's military collapse in November 1918, chaotic workers' and soldiers' councils proliferated. One of Einstein's lectures at the University of Berlin was 'cancelled due to revolution.' On November 16, Einstein was one of the original signers of a manifesto announcing the creation of a progressive middle-class party, the German Democratic Party. After a democratically elected assembly met in Weimar, Einstein formally accepted German citizenship as a gesture of support for the infant republic.

With his scientific fame, Einstein could act as unofficial spokesman for the Weimar Republic and he protested against the continued hostility of Germany's former enemies. In 1921, he refused to attend the third Solvay Congress in Belgium, since all other German scientists were excluded from it. In 1922, he joined a newly created Committee on Intellectual Cooperation setup under the League of Nations. The next year he resigned, distressed by the League's impotence when confronted with France's occupation of the German Ruhr. But he soon returned to the committee. As a leading member of the German League for Human Rights, he worked hard for better relations with France. He also made numerous gestures against militarism.

Einstein attracted attention to a number of causes, such as the release of political prisoners and the defence of democracy against the spread of fascism. He spoke in public, made statements to the press, signed petitions. In 1924, he defended the radical Bauhaus School of Architecture. In 1927, he signed a protest against Italian fascism. In 1929, he appealed for the commutation of death sentences given to Arab rioters in British Palestine.

# CHAPTER 10
# A Busy Phase

Although Einstein was regarded warily in Berlin, such was the demand for him in other European cities that he travelled widely to lecture on relativity, usually arriving at each place by third-class rail carriage, with a violin tucked under his arm. He went to various countries as a spokesman for liberal causes and as a scientist. People looked upon him as an esteemed member of the physics community.

His lectures were extremely successful. On one occasion, an enthusiastic impresario guaranteed him a three-week booking at the London Palladium. He ignored the offer but, at the request of the Zionist leader Chaim Weizmann, toured the United States in 1921 to raise money for the Palestine Foundation Fund. Frequently treated like a circus freak and feted from morning to night, Einstein nevertheless was gratified by the standards of scientific research and the 'idealistic attitudes' that he found prevailing in the United States.

During the next three years Einstein was constantly on the move. He journeyed not only to European capitals but also to Asia, to the Middle East and to South America. According to his diary notes, he found nobility among the Hindus of Ceylon (now Sri Lanka), a purity of soul among the Japanese and a magnificent intellectual and moral calibre among the Jewish settlers in Palestine. His wife later wrote that, on steaming into one new harbour, Einstein had said to her, "Let us take it all in before we wake up."

In Shanghai, a cable reached him announcing that he had been awarded the 1921 Nobel Prize for Physics, "for your photoelectric law and your work in the field of theoretical Physics." However, relativity, which was still the centre of controversy, was not mentioned. In 1922, he went to Sweden to accept the Nobel Prize.

Though the 1920s were tumultuous times of wide acclaim and some notoriety, Einstein did not waver from his new search. He continued working for finding the mathematical relationship between electromagnetism and gravitation. This would be a first step, he felt, in discovering the common laws governing the behaviour of even-thing in the universe, from the electron to the planets. He sought to relate the universal properties of matter and energy in a single equation or formula, in what came to be called a Unified Field Theory. This turned out to be a fruitless quest that occupied the rest of his life.

# CHAPTER 11
# Developing Quantum Theory and Einstein

Einstein's peers generally agreed quite early that his search was destined to fail. They reasoned that the rapidly developing quantum theory uncovered an uncertainty principle in all measurements of the motion of particles. The new theory advocated that the movement of a single particle simply could not be predicted because of a fundamental uncertainty in measuring simultaneously both its speed and its position, which means, in effect, that the future of any physical system at the subatomic level cannot be predicted. While fully recognising the brilliance of quantum mechanics, Einstein rejected the idea that these theories were absolute and persevered with his theory of general relativity as the more satisfactory foundation to future discovery. He was widely quoted on his belief in an exactly engineered universe, "God is subtle but he is not malicious." On this point, he parted company with most theoretical physicists. The distinguished German quantum theorist Max Born, a close friend of Einstein, said at the time, "Many of us regard this as a tragedy, both for him, as he gropes his way in loneliness and for us, who miss our leader and standard-bearer." This appraisal and others, pronouncing his work in later life as largely wasted effort, had to await the judgment of later generations.

The year 1929, which marked Einstein's 50th birthday, denoted the beginning of the ebb and flow of his life's work in a number of aspects. Early in the year, the Prussian Academy published the first version of his unified field theory. However, despite the sensation it caused, its very preliminary nature soon became apparent. The reception of the theory left him undaunted, but Einstein was dismayed by the preludes to certain disaster in the field of human affairs.

Anti-Semitism was openly pursued by the powerful political right and the emerging Nazi party since 1919. Nazi physicists and their followers violently denounced Einstein's theory of relativity as 'Jewish-Communist physics'. At times his friends feared for his safety. Such anti-Semitism was one reason why Einstein, although he believed in world government rather than nationalism, gave public support to Zionism. "In so far as a particular community is attacked as such" he said, "it is bound to defend itself as such, so that its individual members may be able to maintain their material and spiritual interests... In present circumstances, the rebuilding of Palestine is the only object that has a sufficiently strong appeal to stimulate the Jews to effective corporate action."

# CHAPTER 12
# Changing Human Affairs

A law in Berlin required Einstein to join the official Jewish religious community in the country. Refusing to succumb to the law, he said, "Much as I feel myself a Jew, I feel far removed from traditional religious forms."

However, crushing Einstein's natural gaiety more than any of these events was the mental breakdown of his younger son, Edward. Edward had worshipped his father from a distance, but now blamed him for deserting him and for ruining his life. Einstein's sorrow was eased only slightly by the amicable relationship he enjoyed with his older son, Hans Albert.

Between 1930 and 1933, Einstein spent each winter in Pasadena at the California Institute of Technology, each spring in Berlin and each summer near Berlin in a home at Caputh. The changing circumstances around him left him longing for a composed environment. On one occasion, he said, "How I wish that somewhere there existed an island for those who are wise and of goodwill! In such a place even I would be an ardent patriot."

In 1931, as a visiting professor at the University of Oxford, Einstein spent as much time espousing pacifism as he did discussing science. He went so far as to authorise the establishment of the Einstein War Resisters' International Fund in order to bring massive public pressure to bear on the World Disarmament Conference. The conference was scheduled in Geneva in February 1932. When these talks foundered, Einstein felt that his years of supporting world peace and human understanding had accomplished nothing. Bitterly disappointed, he visited Geneva to focus world attention on the 'farce' of the disarmament conference. In a rare moment of fury, Einstein stated to a journalist, "They [the politicians and statesmen] have cheated us. They have fooled us. Hundreds of millions of people in Europe and in America, billions of men and women yet to be born, have been and are being cheated, traded and cricked out of their lives and health and well-being."

# CHAPTER 13
# Discourses with Great Minds

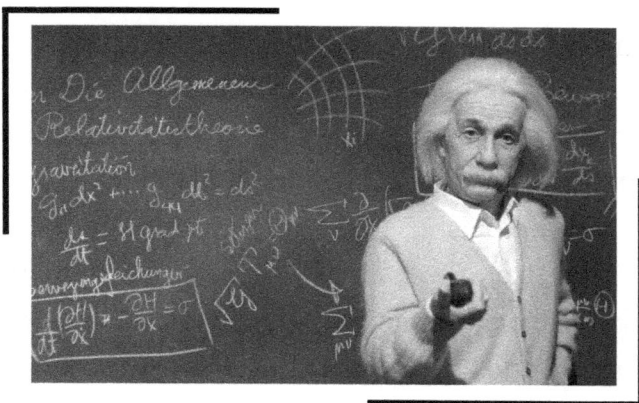

Shortly after Einstein went to Germany, he started writing to the famous Austrian psychiatrist Sigmund Freud. In his letters, Einstein suggested that people must have an innate lust for hatred and destruction. Freud agreed, adding that war was biologically sound because of the love-hate instincts of man and that pacifism was an idiosyncrasy directly related to

Einstein's high degree of cultural development. This exchange was only one of Einstein's many philosophic dialogues with renowned men of his age.

With Rabindranath Tagore, Hindu poet and mystic, he discussed the nature of truth. While Tagore held that truth was realised through man, Einstein maintained that scientific truth must be conceived as a valid truth that is independent of humanity. "I cannot prove that I am right in this, but that is my religion," said Einstein. Firmly denying atheism, Einstein expressed a belief in "Spinoza's God, who reveals himself in the harmony of what exists." The physicist's breadth of spirit and depth of enthusiasm were always most evident among truly intellectual men. He loved being with the physicists Paul Ehrenfest and Hendrik A. Lorentz at Netherlands' Leiden University and several times he visited the California Institute of Technology in Pasadena to attend seminars at the Mt. Wilson Observatory, which had become world renowned as a centre for astrophysical research.

At Mt. Wilson, Einstein heard that the Belgian scientist Abbe Georges Lemaitre detailed his theory that the universe had been created by the explosion of a 'primeval atom' and was still expanding. Gleefully, Einstein jumped to his feet, applauding. "This is the most beautiful and satisfactory explanation of creation to which I have ever listened," he said.

In 1933, soon after Adolf Hitler became chancellor of Germany, Einstein renounced his German citizenship and left the country. Many universities abroad were eager to invite the renowned scientist. He later accepted a full-time position as a foundation member of the school of mathematics at the new Institute for Advanced Study in Princeton, New Jersey. In reprisal, Nazi storm troopers ransacked his beloved summerhouse at Caputh, near Berlin and confiscated his sailboat. Einstein was so convinced that Nazi Germany was preparing for war that, to the horror of Remain Holland and his other pacifist friends, he violated his pacifist ideals and urged free Europe to arm and recruit for defence.

Although his warnings about war were largely ignored, there were fears for Einstein's life. He was taken by private yacht from Belgium to England. By the time he arrived in Princeton in October 1933, he had noticeably aged. A friend wrote, "It was as if something had deadened in him. He sat in a chair at our place, twisting his white hair in his fingers and talking dreamily about everything under the sun. He was not laughing any more.

# CHAPTER 14
# Einstein's Public Activities during 1930-35

During a stay in England in September 1933, Einstein met Winston Churchill, Lloyd George and prominent British scientists and intellectuals. He tried to warn them of the Nazi danger. Many noted academicians were fleeing Germany, few of them received abroad as warmly as Einstein. He worked on behalf of the Emergency Committee to Aid Displaced German Scholars and other organisations that tried to find homes for both Jewish and political refugees.

*1930*

- With Stefan Zweig, Bertrand Russell and others, signs petition favouring the Kellogg-Briand arms limitation pact.

- Appeals against conscription and military training of young men; signs petition with Thomas Mann, Romain Rolland, and others.
- Speaks at the New History Society, New York, translated by the pacifist Rosika Schwimtr.

*1931*

- Attends special screening in Hollywood of "All Quiet on the Western front", a film banned in Germany; supports the German League for Human Rights campaign to have the film shown in Germany.
- Speaks at the California Institute of Technology on the social role of science.
- Addresses a peace group at Chicago railway station.
- Joins an international protest to save lives of eight Scottsboro, Alabama blacks wrongly convicted of rape.
- Speaks at a mass protest meeting supporting Grumbel, a liberal professor under attack in Germany.

- Supports the International Union of Anti-militarist Clergymen and Ministers, who call for a Geneva peace conference.
- Speaks at a student meeting of League of The Nations Association.
- Meets with War Resisters International; sends message to their conference in France.

*1931*

- Attends meeting of the Los Angeles University of International Relations.
- Speaks to the Joint Peace Council, with Lord Ponsonby, on the failure of disarmament conferences.
- Exchanges letters with Freud under auspices of International Institute of Intellectual Cooperation, leading to publication of pamphlet, 'Why War?"

*1933*

- Addresses student group at the California Institute of Technology in Pasadena.
- Resigns from the Prussian and Bavarian Academies of Science in protest after Hitler takes power; in open letter, he denies the

accusation that he spread propaganda on anti-Semitic atrocities.

- Accepts election as a Founding
- Member, with Lord Davies, of the New Commonwealth Society; discusses international army and navy police force.
- Speaks at a mass meeting in London for the Refugee Assistance Fund to aid victims of the Nazis.
- Guest of honour at the World Peaceways dinner in New York.

*1934*

- Speaks at a Princeton, New Jersey state conference on Causes and Cures of War.
- Sends letter to the Anti-War Committee at New York University.
- Makes national radio speech on Brotherhood Day, sponsored by National Conference of Christians and Jews.
- Sends message to the Educators and World Peace conference of the Progressive Education Association in New York.

*1935*

- With Alfred E. Smith, speaks on national radio and at a New York dinner to aid political and non-Jewish refugees from Germany.
- Helps to initiate campaign for a Nobel Peace Prize for the pacifist Carl von Ossietzky, then ill in a German concentration camp.
- With John Dewey and Alvin Johnson, becomes member of the United States of the International League for Academic Freedom.
- Speaks at Passover celebration in at the Manhattan Opera House, urging Jewish-Arab amity in Palestine.

# CHAPTER 15
# Later Years in The United States

In Princeton, Einstein set a pattern that was to vary little for more than 20 years. He lived with his wife in a simple, two-story frame house and most mornings walked a mile or so to the Institute, where he worked on his unified field theory and talked with colleagues. For relaxation, he played his violin and sailed on a local lake. Only rarely did he travel, even to New York. In a letter to Queen Elizabeth of Belgium, he described his new refuge as a "wonderful little spot... a quaint and ceremonious village of puny demigods on stilts."

Eventually he acquired American citizenship, but he always continued to think of himself as a European. Pursuing his own line of theoretical research outside the mainstream of Physics, he took on an air of fixed serenity. "Among my European friends, I am now called *Der grosse Schweiger* ("The Great Stone Face"), a title I well deserve," he said.

In 1936, his wife Elsa died. One of her daughters and Einstein's long-time secretary lived on with Einstein in Princeton and helped with housekeeping. Even his wife's death did not disturb Einstein's outward calm. "It seemed that the difference between life and death for Einstein consisted only in the difference between being able and not being able to do Physics," wrote Leopold Infield, the Polish physicist who arrived in Princeton at that time. Niels Bohr, the great Danish atomic physicist, brought news to Einstein in 1939 that the German refugee physicist Lise Meitner had split the uranium atom, with a slight loss of total mass that had been converted into energy. Meitner's experiments, performed in Copenhagen, had been inspired by similar, though less precise, experiments done months earlier in Berlin by two German chemists, Otto Hahn and Fritz Strassmann. Bohr speculated that if an uncontrolled chain-reaction splitting of uranium atoms could be accomplished, a mammoth explosion would result. Einstein was skeptical, but laboratory experiments in the United States showed the feasibility of the idea. With an European war regarded as imminent, it was feared that Nazi scientists might build such a "bomb" first, Einstein was persuaded by colleagues to write a letter to President Franklin D. Roosevelt urging "watchfulness and, if necessary, quick action" on the part of the United States in atomic-bomb research. This recommendation marked the beginning of the Manhattan Project.

# CHAPTER 16
# Final Years

Although Einstein took no part in the work at Los Alamos, New Mexico and did not learn that a nuclear-fission bomb had been made until Hiroshima was razed in 1945, his name was emphatically associated with the advent of the atomic age. He readily joined those scientists seeking ways to prevent any future use of the bomb, his particular and urgent plea being the establishment of a world government under a constitution drafted by the United States, Britain and Russia. With the spur of the atomic fear that haunted the world, he said "we must not be merely willing, but actively eager to submit ourselves to the binding authority necessary for world security." Once more, Einstein emerged in newspaper headlines. Letters and statements tumbled out of his Princeton study and in the public eye Einstein, the physicist, dissolved into Einstein the world citizen, a kind 'grand old man' devoting his last years to bringing harmony to the world.

The rejection of his ideals by statesmen and politicians did not break him, because his prime obsession still remained with physics. "I cannot tear myself away from my work," he wrote at the time. "It has me inexorably in its clutches." In proof of this came his new version of the unified field in 1950, a most meticulous mathematical essay that was immediately but politely criticised by most physicists as untenable.

Compared with his renown of a generation earlier, Einstein was virtually neglected and said himself that he felt almost like a stranger in the world. His health deteriorated to the extent that he could no longer play the violin or sail his boat. Many years earlier, chronic abdominal pains had forced him to give up smoking his pipe and to watch his diet carefully.

Einstein died in his sleep at Princeton Hospital. On his desk lay his last incomplete statement, written to honour Israeli Independence Day.

It read in part: "What I seek to accomplish is simply to serve with my feeble capacity truth and justice at the risk of pleasing no one." His contribution to man's understanding of the universe was matchless and he is established for all time as a giant of Science. Broadly speaking, his crusades in human affairs seem to have no lasting impact. Einstein perhaps anticipated such an assessment of his life when he said, "Politics are for the moment. An equation is for eternity."

# CHAPTER 17
# The 1932 Disarmament Conference

The following are excerpts from an article Einstein wrote in 1931 for the Disarmament Conference:

What the inventive genius of mankind has bestowed upon us in the last hundred years, could have made human life care free and happy if the development of the organising power of man had been able to keep step with his technical advances. Worst of all is the technical development, which produces the means for the destruction of human life and the dearly created products of labour. We older people lived through that shuddering in the World War. But even more terrible than this destruction seems to me the unworthy servitude into which the individual is swept by war. Is it not terrible to be forced by the community to deeds, which every individual feels to be most despicable crimes? Only a few have had the moral greatness to resist; they are in my eyes the true heroes of the World War.

The failure of the conference would be assured if the delegates were to arrive in Geneva with fixed instructions and aims, the achievement of which would at once become a matter of national prestige. This seems to be universally recognised, for the meetings of the statesmen of any two states, of which we have seen a number of late, have been utilised for discussions of the problem of disarmament in order to clear the ground for the conference. This procedure seems to me a very happy one, for two persons, or two groups, ordinarily conduct themselves most sensibly, most honourably and with the greatest freedom from passion if no third person listens in, whom the others believe they must consider or conciliate in their speeches. We can only hope for a favourable outcome in this most vital conference if the meeting is prepared for exhaustively in this way by advance discussions in order that surprises shall be made impossible and if, through honest goodwill, an atmosphere of mutual confidence and trust can be effectively created in advance.

Success in such great affairs is not a matter of cleverness, or even shrewdness, but instead a matter of honourable conduct and mutual confidence. You cannot substitute intellect for moral conduct in this matter—I should like to say, thank God that you cannot!

# CHAPTER 18
# Excerpts from 'The World As I See It'

*The World as I see it*

What an extraordinary situation is that of us mortals! Each of us is here for a brief sojourn; for what purpose he knows not, though he sometimes thinks he feels it, ".... A hundred times even- day I remind myself that my inner and outer life depend on the labours of other men, living and dead and that I must exert myself in order to give in the same measure as I have received and am still receiving. I am strongly drawn to the simple life and am often oppressed by the feeling that I am engrossing an unnecessary amount of the labour of my fellow-men... Everybody acts not only under external compulsion but also in accordance with inner necessity. Schopenhauer's saying, that "a man can do as he will, but not will as he will" has been an inspiration to me since my youth up and a continual consolation and unfailing well-spring of patience in the face of the hardships of life, my own and others." This feeling mercifully mitigates the sense of responsibility which so easily becomes paralysing and it prevents us from taking ourselves and other people too seriously; it conduces to a view of life in which humour, above all, has its due place.

*Mysterious*

The fairest thing we can experience is the mysterious. It is the fundamental emotion, which stands at the cradle of true art and true science. He who knows it not and can no longer wonder, no longer feel amazement, is as good as dead, a snuffed-out candle. It was the experience of mystery—even if mixed with fear-that engendered religion... I cannot conceive of a God who rewards and punishes his creatures, or has a will of the type of which we are conscious in ourselves. An individual who should survive his physical death is also beyond my comprehension, nor do I wish it otherwise; such notions are for the fears or absurd egoism of feeble souls. Enough for me the mystery of the eternity of life and the inkling of the marvellous structure of reality, together with the single-hearted endeavour to comprehend a portion, is it never so tiny, of the reason that manifests itself in nature.

# CHAPTER 19
# Einstein on the Meaning of Life

The following are excerpts from a letter written by Einstein in response to a 19-year-old Rutger's University student, who had written to Einstein of his despair at seeing no visible purpose to life and no help from religion. In responding to this poignant cry for help, Einstein offered no easy solace and this very fact must have heartened the student and lightened the lonely burden of his doubts. Here is Einstein's response. It was written in English and sent from Princeton on 3 December 1950, "within days of receiving the letter I was impressed by the earnestness of your struggle to find a purpose for the life of the individual and of mankind as a whole. In my opinion there can be no reasonable answer if the question is put this way. If we speak of the purpose and goal of an action we mean simply the question: which kind of desire should we fulfill by the action or its consequences or which undesired consequences should be prevented-We can, of course, also speak in a clear way of the goal of an action from the standpoint of a community to which the individual belongs. In such cases the goal of the action has also to do at least indirectly with fulfillment of desires of the individuals, which constitute a society.

If you ask for the purpose or goal of society as a whole or of an individual taken as a whole the question loses its meaning. This is, of course, even more so if you ask the purpose or meaning of nature in general. For in those cases it seems quite arbitrary if not unreasonable to assume somebody whose desires are connected with the happenings. Nevertheless we all feel that it is indeed very reasonable and important to ask ourselves how we should try to conduct our lives. The answer is, in my opinion: satisfaction of the desires and needs of all, as far as this can be achieved and achievement of harmony and beauty in the human relationships. This presupposes a good deal of conscious thought and of self-education. It is undeniable that the enlightened Greeks and the old Oriental sages had achieved a higher level in this all-important field than what is alive in our schools and universities."

# CHAPTER 20
# Becoming a Free Thinker and a Scientist

The following is an excerpt from Einstein's Autobiographical Notes:

"When I was a fairly precocious young man I became thoroughly impressed with the futility of the hopes and strivings that chase most men restlessly through life. Moreover, I soon discovered the cruelty of that chase, which in those years was much more carefully covered up by hypocrisy and glittering words than is the case today. By the mere existence of his stomach everyone was condemned to participate in that chase. The stomach might well be satisfied by such participation, but not man insofar as he is a thinking and feeling being."

"As the first way out there was religion, which is implanted into every child by way of the traditional education-machine. Thus I came -though the child of entirely irreligious (Jewish) parents - to a deep religiousness, which, however, reached an abrupt end at the age of twelve. Through the reading of popular scientific books I soon reached the conviction that much in the stories of the Bible could not be true. The consequence was a positively fanatic orgy of freethinking coupled with the impression that youth is intentionally being deceived by the state through lies; it was a crushing impression. Mistrust of every kind of authority grew out of this experience, a sceptical attitude toward the convictions that were alive in any specific social environment-an attitude that has never again left me, even though, later on, it has been tempered by a better insight into the causal connections. It is quite clear to me that the religious paradise of youth, which was thus lost, was the first attempt to free myself from the chains of the "merely personal," from an existence dominated by wishes, hopes and primitive feelings. Out yonder there was this huge world, which exists independently of us human beings and which stands before us like a great, eternal riddle, at least partially accessible to our inspection and thinking. The contemplation of this world beckoned as a liberation and I soon noticed that many a man whom I had learned to esteem and to admire had round inner freedom and security in its pursuit. The mental grasp of this extra-personal world within the frame of our capabilities presented itself to my mind, half consciously, half unconsciously, as a supreme goal. Similarly motivated men of the present and of the past, as well as the insights they had achieved, were the friends who could not be lost. The road to this paradise was not as comfortable and alluring as the road to the religious paradise; but it has shown itself reliable and I have never regretted having chosen it."

# CHAPTER 21
# Einstein's Letter to President Franklin Roosevelt

The following is an excerpt of the letter signed by Albert Einstein, which was delivered to President Franklin Roosevelt by Alexander Sachs on October 11,1939. The chief author is believed to be Leo Szilard.

Albert Einstein Old Grove Rd.

Nassau Point

Peconic, Long Island

August 2nd, 1939

ED. Roosevelt

President of the United States

White House

Washington, D.C. Sir:

Some recent work by E. Fermi and L.

Szilard, which has been communicated to me in manuscript, leads me to expect that the element uranium may be turned into a new and important source of energy in the immediate future... I believe therefore that it is my duty to bring to your attention the following facts and recommendations. In the course of the last four months it has been made probable—through the work of Joliot in France as well as Fermi and Szilard in America—that it may become possible to set up a nuclear chain reaction in a large mass of uranium...

This new phenomenon would also lead to the construction of bombs and it is conceivable—though much less certain—that extremely powerful bombs of a new type may thus be constructed. A single bomb of this type, carried by boat and exploded in a port, might very well destroy the whole port together with some of the surrounding territory. However, such bombs might very well prove to be too heavy for transportation by air.

The United States has only very poor ores of uranium in moderate quantities. There is good ore in Canada and the former Czechoslovakia, while the most important source of uranium is the Belgian Congo.

In view of this situation you may think it desirable to have some permanent contact maintained between the Administration and the group of physicists working on chain reactions in America. One possible way of achieving this might be for you to entrust with this task a person who has your confidence who could perhaps serve in an unofficial capacity. His task might comprise the following:

(a) To approach Government Departments, keep them informed of the further development and put forward recommendations for Government action, giving particular attention to the problems of securing a supply of uranium ore for the United States.

(b) To speed up the experimental work, which is at present being carried on within the limits of the budgets of University laboratories, by providing funds, if such funds be required, through his contacts with private persons who are willing to make contributions for this cause and perhaps also by obtaining the co-operation of industrial laboratories which have the necessary equipment.

I understand that Germany has actually stopped the sale of uranium from the Czechoslovakian mines, which she has taken over. That she should have taken such early action might perhaps be understood on the ground that the son of the German Under-Secretary of State, Von Weizaecker, is attached to the Kaiser-Wilhelm-Institute in Berlin where some of the American work on uranium is now being repeated.

Yours very truly

A. Einstein

# CHAPTER 22
# Nobel Prize Acceptance Speech

Albert Einstein received The Nobel Prize in Physics in the year 1921 for his outstanding, contribution to the field of Physics. In 1923, he delivered a lecture to the Nordiac Assembly of Naturalists at Gothenburg as his Nobel Prize acceptance speech. The following are excerpts from Einstein's Nobel Prize acceptance speech *Fundamental ideas and problems of the theory of relativity*

**July 11,1923**

If we consider that part of the theory of relativity, which may nowadays in a sense be regarded as bonafide scientific knowledge, we note two aspects which have a major bearing on this theory. The whole development of the theory turns on the question of whether there are physically preferred states of motion in Nature (physical relativity problem). Also, concepts and distinctions are only admissible to the extent that observable facts can be assigned to them without ambiguity (stipulation that concepts and distinctions should have meaning). This postulate, pertaining to epistemology, proves to be of fundamental importance.

I am mentioning these deficiencies of method because in the same sense they are also a feature of the relativity theory in the schematic exposition which I am advocating here. Certainly it would be logically more correct to begin with the whole of the laws and to apply the 'stipulation of meaning' to this whole first, i.e. to put the unambiguous relation to the world of experience last instead of already fulfilling it in an imperfect form for an artificially isolated part, namely the space-time metric.

We are not, however, sufficiently advanced in our knowledge of Nature's elementary laws to adopt this more perfect method without going out of our depth. At the close of our considerations, we shall see that in the most recent studies there is an attempt, based on ideas by Levi-Civita, Weyl and Eddington, to implement that logically purer method.

The special Theory of Relativity is an adaptation of physical principles to Maxwell-Lorentz electrodynamics. From earlier physics it takes the assumption that Euclidian geometry is valid for the laws governing the position of rigid bodies, the inertial frame and the law of inertia. The postulate of equivalence of inertial frames for the formulation of the laws of Nature is assumed to be valid for the whole of physics (special relativity principle). From Maxwell-Lorentz electrodynamics, it takes the postulate of invariance of the velocity of light in a vacuum (light principle).

# CHAPTER 23
# Albert Einstein's Quotations

Learn from yesterday, live for today, hope for tomorrow. The important thing is not to stop questioning.

Albert Einstein

- Common sense is the collection of prejudices acquired by age eighteen.
- God does not care about our mathematical difficulties. He integrates empirically.
- What is this frog and mouse battle among the mathematicians?
- God is subtle, but he is not malicious.

- Nature hides her secrets because of her essential loftiness, but not by means of ruse.
- The human mind has first to construct forms, independently, before we can find them in things.
- Since the mathematicians have invaded the theory of relativity, I do not understand it myself anymore.
- The truth of a theory is in your mind, not in your eyes.
- These thoughts did not come in any verbal formulation. I rarely think in words at all. A thought comes and I may try to express it in words afterward.
- The world needs heroes and its better they be harmless men like me than villains like Hitler.
- It is nothing short of a miracle that modern methods of instruction have not yet entirely strangled the holy curiosity of inquiry.
- The search for truth is more precious than its possession.
- If my theory of relativity is proven successful, Germany will claim me as a German and

France will declare that I am a citizen of the world. Should my theory prove untrue, France will say that I am a German and Germany will declare that I am a Jew.

- When I am judging a theory, I ask myself whether, if I were God, I would have arranged the world in such a way.

- But the creative principle resides in mathematics. In a certain sense, therefore, I hold true that pure thought can grasp reality, as the ancients dreamed.

- But there is another reason for the high repute of mathematics: it is mathematics that offers the exact natural sciences a certain measure of security which, without mathematics, they could not attain.

- One reason why mathematics enjoys special esteem, above all other sciences, is that its laws are absolutely certain and indisputable, while those of other sciences are to some extent debatable and in constant danger of being overthrown by newly discovered facts.

# CHAPTER 24
# Chronology

1879  Born in Ulm, Germany

1880  Moves to Munich.

1888  Enters Luitpold School in Munich.

1894  Family moves to Italy, Albert stays at Luitpold.

1895  Rejoins family in Pavia, then goes to cantonal school in Aarau, Switzerland.

1896  Renounces German citizenship. Gets diploma from Aarau, enrolls at ETH (Federal Institute of Technology) in Zurich.

1900  Gets diploma from ETH.

1901  Becomes Swiss citizen.

1902  Employed at patent office, Bern.

1903  Marries Mileva Maric (1875-1948).

1905  Publishes in the *Annalen der Physik*

1909  Becomes associate professor at University

of Zurich. Further work on quantum theory.

1911 Becomes full professor at Karl-Ferdinand University in Prague. Predicts bending of starlight at eclipses (but gets the magnitude wrong).

1912 Becomes professor at the ETH in Zurich.

1914 Becomes professor at University of Berlin. Separates from Mileva. Outbreak of First World War. ,

1915 Cosigns "Manifesto to Europeans" separating himself from German militarism.

*-Feldgleichungen der Gravitation*, the general relativity equations.

1916 Becomes president of the German Physical Society.

1918 End of First World War; revolution in Germany.

1919 Divorced from Mileva. Marries his cousin Elsa Einstein Lowenthal (1876-1936). Her adult daughters by a previous marriage, Ilse (1897-1934) and Margot

(1899-1986), had already legally taken the name Einstein.

Bending of light near sun observed at eclipse.

1920 Public attacks on relativity theory and Einstein by anti-Semites.

1921 First visit to United States.

1922 Works on unified field theory. Awarded Nobel Prize in Physics.

1927 Begins dialogue on quantum theory interpretation with Niels Bohr.

1930 Extended visit to United States, chiefly at the California Institute of Technology.

1932 Appointed professor at Institute for Advanced Study, Princeton.

1933 Nazis come to power in Germany; Einstein settles in United States.

1936 Death of Elsa.

1939 Outbreak of Second World War; Einstein signs letter to President Roosevelt warning of possibility of atomic bombs.

1940 Becomes citizen of United States (retaining Swiss citizenship).

1945  Atomic bombing of Hiroshima and Nagasaki; end of Second World War.

1946  Serves as chairman of Emergency Committee of Atomic Scientists.

1948  Generalised theory of gravitation, an example of continuing attempts to find a more universal mathematical approach to field theory.

1952  Declines offered presidency of Israel.

1955  (April 18) Dies in Princeton.

www.ingramcontent.com/pod-product-compliance
Lightning Source LLC
LaVergne TN
LVHW041305080426
835510LV00009B/871